50 IRS Audit Flags
and
How to Avoid Them

JASON KNICKERBOCKER

CONTENTS

INTRODUCTION

If you self-prepare your own taxes, or if you hire a tax accountant, this book is an informative guide to help lower your overall risk of an IRS audit.

Whether you are a business owner with complicated taxes or a W-2 employee with simple taxes, it's a good idea to try and avoid an audit.

An audit will at a minimum cost you time but could also end up costing you money. In a worst-case scenario, an IRS audit could even land you in jail.

This book is a quick and easy read to help you try and avoid an audit for tax years 2024 and 2025. I will update this book every few years so it can be used in conjunction with your tax strategy. I purposely did not include a lot of fluff or fancy words. First of all, I am a retired street cop, so I have to look most fancy words up. More importantly, I want you to be able to skim through this book in an hour or so and come out with some basic knowledge of audit risks.

This book is just one piece of the puzzle. With this book and with some tax planning and research, you can legally lower your overall tax bill.

ABOUT THE AUTHOR

In my opinion, it is important to know who is talking, so I am going to step outside my comfort zone and tell you a little bit about myself.

I took a unique path to get to where I am, and because my path was different than most tax accountants, I feel I can explain the tax code in an easy-to-understand manner. Most books on IRS topics are boring 200-page manuals, and my goal is to be a less boring 99-page manual!

OK so here we go! I went to the University of Arizona where I obtained a bachelor's degree in business administration. Right out of college, instead of going into business, I decided to pursue my childhood dream of becoming a cop. At the age of twenty-two, I became as a deputy sheriff in Tucson, Arizona and after a few years, I moved to California and became a police officer in Manhattan Beach, California.

I spent about twenty-one years total in law enforcement, including time on patrol, as a detective, riding a police motorcycle, as a SWAT team member and later as a SWAT team commander. I was even blessed enough to become a sergeant and later a lieutenant before I retired. The department I worked for was in a relatively safe area, so compared to other police officers, I don't have as many good war stories. However, I did learn how to read and interpret municipal, state, and federal law. The time I spent reading and interpreting legal books helped prepare me to be a good tax accountant. Most people think taxes are a numbers gig, but it is equally important to know how to read and interpret tax law.

In 2009, while I was a police officer, I signed up for the Army National Guard and served as an infantry platoon leader for just over six years. I never saw combat, which I have mixed feelings about, but I did learn a lot.

In my brief time in the military, I witnessed big government bureaucracy at its finest. I learned that a person on the other end of a keyboard can push a button and fix everything or that they can be lazy and rude and solve nothing. If you have ever called the IRS, you know what I'm talking about! It is sometimes luck of the draw!

Unbeknownst to me at the time, my military education in red tape would prepare me to deal with the IRS later in life as a tax accountant. Not only did I get a crash course on red tape, but I also learned how to follow federal instructions and forms which can be mind-numbing.

At the age of forty-four, I retired from law enforcement and fled California like most retired police officers do. I studied for about two years and became an IRS Enrolled Agent (EA) which is the highest credential the IRS offers. EAs specialize in taxation and are federally authorized tax practitioners who have unlimited rights to represent taxpayers before the IRS in all fifty states.

Currently, I run a small tax practice in Cave Creek, Arizona. We specialize in high-net-worth clients and small to medium businesses. For some unknown reason, I thoroughly enjoy being a tax accountant and reading the tax code. I never saw this in the cards when I was a kid or when I was a cop trying to look cool. Who knows, maybe I hit my head one too many times, but I love it and constantly immerse myself in tax research and tax classes.

Overall, with my government experience, my life experience, my formal education, and owning a tax practice, I feel well-equipped to manage all sorts of tax issues.

Most importantly, I am blessed with four kids and a wife who love and put up with me! We are big on outdoor adventures—hiking, camping, water sports, you name it. We are Christians, and our faith is important to us. We are imperfect, yes, I said IMPERFECT but with God's grace, we get by each day despite all the imperfections we (but especially me) bring to the table.

My love of serving people, teaching and freedom inspired me to write this book. I want to share my experiences and help others avoid a battle with the IRS. If you get something out of this book to help you avoid the IRS sending you an audit letter, then I have done my job.

THE MYSTERIOUS IRS DIF SCORE

Before we can start with the list I have compiled of IRS audit red flags, I need to briefly talk about the mysterious DIF score. You probably have never heard of the DIF score, but if you are diving into the world of taxation, it is important for you to know about.

DIF stands for Discriminant Index Function, and it is a computer-generated score that assesses the risk of inaccuracies in your tax return. When you file your taxes, your tax return is scanned by the IRS's lean and mean DIF computer. The DIF computer kicks out a score which will in part decide your fate regarding an audit. The exact formula for calculating the DIF score is one of the IRS's best-kept secrets.

What you need to know for this book is, the higher your DIF score, the more likely your return will be flagged for further examination by a human. Once it is pulled and looked at by a human, that person will either send it for audit or let it go back onto the pile of tax returns without an audit.

Your goal, after reading this book, should be to stay under the radar and never have your tax return score high enough on the

DIF computer to be looked at by a human. In addition, if and when your tax return is looked at by a human, you want to appear to be reasonable and honest and have it put back onto the pile of tax returns not sent for audit.

There is a very good book called "How to Beat the I.R.S. at Its Own Game: Strategies to Avoid—And Survive—An Audit" by mathematician Amir D. Aczel. I highly recommend his book if you want more detailed information on the mysterious DIF score.

On a side note, I am quite sure by writing this book, I will be audited within a year or two!

DATA SOURCES

I have researched and included some of the most recently published audit rates, but I am not a researcher by trade. I am a retired cop turned tax guy, and my data comes from various and sometimes weird sources.

I relied on my knowledge from studying to become an Enrolled Agent, tax returns I have prepared that were later audited, IRS classes, continuing education classes, tax books, IRS reports to congress, college tax classes, and tax conventions.

While conducting research for this book, I talked to a lot of people such sober IRS agents, drunk IRS agents, real estate investors, real estate agents, IRS instructors, my 80-year-old uncle who owns a CPA firm in Beverly Hills, payroll providers, tax attorneys, IRS appeal examiners, bankers, fraud investigators, mortgage brokers, people who have been through rough audits and numerous business owners.

In addition to collecting data from human sources, I also obtained data from things such as Google, ChatGPT, on-line tax forums, professional tax membership organizations, tax newsletters I subscribe to and even good old YouTube. I even included some of my own gut feelings and intuition which I have developed by serving in law enforcement for over twenty years.

Few people really know actual IRS audit rates. To me, even some of the numbers the IRS publishes are suspect. The IRS's underlying goal when reporting their "official" audit rates to Congress is to obtain more funding and/or not have the commissioner replaced, aka fired. From my experience, it is not unheard of for government agencies to "adjust" numbers or statistics to fit their narrative or goal.

What I am trying to say is, take the numbers and percentages I have listed as more of an educated guess than statistical certainties. Use this book as one of many tools when filing your taxes.

CHAPTER 1
HIGH INCOME

Why it is a red flag: Making a ton of money makes you a better payoff in terms of time and money for the IRS. Think about it in terms of actual dollars. If you are a high-income earner, and the IRS catches you doing something wrong, they will likely recover more money than they would from a low-income earner.

Recent audit rate: According to recently published IRS data, individuals earning $1 million or more have an audit rate of around 3.2%.

How to protect against it: You can't unless you want to make less money. Just be aware you have about a 3 out of 100 chance of being audited so keep it kosher.

Pro tip: If you itemize your deductions or have various sources of income, you will save money by hiring a good tax accountant. Remember, tax planning can help you avoid taxes, and tax planning is legal.

CHAPTER 2
INCORRECTLY CLAIMING DEPENDENTS

Why it is a red flag: The IRS data matches dependents and will kick it back if two people claim the same dependent.

Recent audit rate: In my experience, it will get rejected by the IRS 100% of the time if someone has already claimed a dependent.

How to protect against it: Talk to your baby's daddy, make a plan, and stick with it.

Pro tip: One of my clients is a great human being and adopted four kids from a drug-addicted parent. The drug-addicted parent is not in their life yet tries to get the child tax credit every year.

My advice to my client is to file right away so the drug-addicted parent cannot get the credit. File first and let the other parent deal with the stress of trying to fix it.

CHAPTER 3
HOME OFFICE DEDUCTION

Why it is a red flag: Claiming a home office is frequently exaggerated.

Recent audit rate: Home office deductions have a published audit rate of approximately 2.7%. I think audit rates will go down though because more people work from home every year.

How to protect against it: Make sure your home office is exclusively used for business and pick a reasonable number.

Pro tip: If you run a website-building business, you likely only need one room which might be 20% of your home. If you sell gym equipment from your home, then maybe you will use your garage and office and can claim 40% of your home. If you claim more than 50% of your home, that is hard to justify and will be looked at more closely.

CHAPTER 4
RENTAL LOSSES

Why it is a red flag: Reporting rental losses, particularly if you don't qualify as a real estate professional, can trigger an audit.

Recent audit rate: If you claim rental losses and have a W-2 job, get ready for an audit. I would say this is a 50/50 roll of the dice. If you don't have a W-2 job, published rates for rental losses are about 2.1%.

How to protect against it: Don't say you are a real estate professional if you also have a W-2 job making $150,000 a year. It is hard to prove the hours required by IRS regulations if you also work 40 hours a week at another job.

Pro tip: If your spouse doesn't work, have them get their real-estate license and have them manage the properties because you can save a lot of money on taxes.

CHAPTER 5
PARTNERSHIP TAX RETURNS WITH LARGE LOSSES

Why it is a red flag: I attended the IRS convention in San Diego at the end of 2023. The IRS commissioner was there, and he spoke to the attendees at several different classes.

In a roundabout way, he said the IRS believes a small percentage of partnership tax returns are illegal tax shelters that conduct zero actual business. He went on to say the IRS is starting to focus on auditing these with their increased budget starting in 2023 and into 2024 and beyond.

Recent audit rate: Partnership tax returns have an extremely low audit rate of approximately 0.5%. Even though the IRS thinks these are sometimes used to fraudulently save on taxes, they have a tough time keeping up with auditing them because of staffing and the complexities of partnership tax returns.

How to protect against it: Run a business and do not just make things up. Side hustles are common and easy to start these days.

Pro tip: Keep a separate bank account, have a real profit motive, market a product or service, and make some sales even if the result is a net loss. Run a business not an illegal tax shelter.

CHAPTER 6
UNREPORTED INCOME

Why it is a red flag: The IRS receives copies of all the tax forms you get and can data match it to your tax return.

Recent audit rate: In my opinion, the chance of an audit or the IRS catching a form you leave out of your taxes such as a W-2 or 1099 is about 75-100%.

How to protect against it: Keep track of your forms and make sure they all find their way onto your tax return.

Pro tip: The IRS will eventually data-match tax forms and send you a letter saying you missed something and owe them money. Pay now or pay later with penalties and interest.

CHAPTER 7

CLAIMING 100% BUSINESS USE OF VEHICLE

Why it is a red flag: 100% use of a vehicle for business is uncommon. This will create a high DIF score which will likely result in your tax return being looked at by a human IRS agent.

Recent audit rate: In my experience, for single-member LLCs, claiming 100% business use of a vehicle has about a 20% chance of being audited.

How to protect against it: Maintain thorough records to support this claim, including mileage logs and evidence of business use.

Pro tip: Be reasonable. It is rare that a car is used 100% for business unless it's used for a trade such as plumbing or electrical. Keep a detailed log and take photos of your vehicle setup if it is used for work over 50%. Keep in mind you may sell the vehicle and then be audited two years later.

CHAPTER 8
CASH BUSINESSES

Why it is a red flag: Cash is always suspicious to the government. They would get rid of it if they could, and one day probably will.

Recent audit rate: According to what I could find, cash-intensive businesses have an audit rate of around 4.5%.

How to protect against it: Keep records and take pictures. Save deposit slips and use accounting software to track income and expenses.

Pro tip: Not much you can do to avoid an audit so just keep good records.

CHAPTER 9
SIGNIFICANT LOSSES ON SCHEDULE C

Why it is a red flag: Losses on Schedule C are a low-hanging fruit that any auditor can look into. Unlike partnership tax returns or corporations, single-member LLCs which go onto a Schedule C are simple to audit.

Recent audit rate: Published data indicates schedule C filers have an audit rate of about 2.9%. If you take a large business loss, the audit rate will go up to about 9% although the exact rate is hard to find.

How to protect against it: Have a separate bank account. Obtain an EIN and ensure all expenses are legitimate and properly documented. Have a clear profit motive and proof of it.

Pro tip: Shift to a partnership tax return which has a lower audit rate. Do not run a hobby as a business because if the IRS determines it is a hobby, they can disallow 3 years of losses which will result in a huge tax bill.

CHAPTER 10
LARGE CHARITABLE DONATIONS

Why it is a red flag: Donations that are large, relative to your income raise red flags on the DIF computer.

Recent audit rate: This is not published anywhere but the gossip amongst tax accountants is that donations exceeding 3% of income are above the norm and will be audited more frequently.

How to protect against it: Make sure you have proper documentation for all charitable contributions, including receipts and written acknowledgments from the charities.

Pro tip: Take pictures of your donations. Like they say, a picture is worth a thousand words.

CHAPTER 11
ROUND NUMBERS

Why it is a red flag: Round numbers are easy for the DIF computer to pick up and score.

Recent audit rate: Not too sure because round numbers cause a return to be looked at by a human. The human will decide if it will be sent for an audit based on other factors that I am listing in the other questions.

How to protect against it: Don't guess on your expenses, donations, medical bills, property taxes, etc.

Pro tip: If you must guess, don't end every guess with a 0. Mix it up with other numbers. For example, if it is $10 make it $9, if it is $1000, make it $999, etc.

CHAPTER 12
FOREIGN BANK ACCOUNTS

Why it is a red flag: The government is suspicious of foreign money and entities.

Recent audit rate: According to the data I could find, foreign bank account holders have an audit rate of approximately 3.5%. Bank managers I spoke to said foreign money is heavily scrutinized.

How to protect against it: Report your foreign bank accounts and assets. There are usually no tax implications for having foreign assets.

Pro tip: FBAR violations have huge penalties and are closely scrutinized so hire an accountant who knows how to report foreign income and assets. It is not illegal to have foreign money or assets, it is illegal to not report it.

CHAPTER 13
HIGH DEDUCTIONS COMPARED TO INCOME

Why it is a red flag: The IRS will think it is shady if you bring in a ton of money but in the end show no profit for several years in a row.

Recent audit rate: This is DIF score low-hanging fruit. According to data I found on the internet, high deductions relative to income have an audit rate of about 2.4%. Amongst accountants, we think it is much higher.

How to protect against it: Tax plan instead of making up dumb stuff. Get a good tax accountant who can help you legally avoid tax.

Pro tip: Tax avoidance is not illegal, but tax evasion is. Buy real estate, buy rentals, sell stocks at a loss when you can, hire your kids, and max out your 401k but do not just make stuff up.

CHAPTER 14
GAMBLING INCOME

Why it is a red flag: Gambling winnings are a data match via a 1099G. Just because you were drunk when the casino gave you the 1099G and you lost it, does not mean the IRS lost its copy.

Recent audit rate: Gambling winnings are almost always a data match so do not try to bend the rules on this one.

How to protect against it: Keep your 1099G and make sure it ends up on your tax return.

Pro tip: Keep a log of your drunk nights hitting the ATM because, in certain circumstances, you can write off gambling losses. Also, ask the casino to withhold taxes so you do not owe a ton of money at tax time.

CHAPTER 15
LARGE TRAVEL MEALS AND ENTERTAINMENT EXPENSES

Why it is a red flag: Travel, meals and entertainment just look shady. If they are too high, the DIF computer will ensure your tax return is sent for review by a human.

Recent audit rate: Hard to say because they are just part of business expenses but anything more than someone in a similar industry can raise a red flag.

How to protect against it: Be reasonable. IRS agents are smart, and they know people like to claim fun stuff as business expenses. Network with others in your industry and compare notes.

Pro tip: Do not be scared of the IRS but do not be careless. Also, entertainment is not deductible so try to legally classify it as something else like team building, marketing, or meals.

CHAPTER 16
BEING FAMOUS

Why it is a red flag: Anytime the IRS can get some free publicity to keep the public scared of them, they will do it.

Recent audit rate: Martha Stewart, Wesley Snipes, Nicolas Cage, Stephen Baldwin, and even Willie Nelson. Need I say more?

How to protect against it: You need to hire a good tax accountant, if you are famous. You need to declare all income and then take expenses.

Pro tip: Tax plan and hire a good tax accountant do not just "unintentionally" forget to claim money you made.

CHAPTER 17
CLAIMING EARNED INCOME TAX CREDIT (EITC)

Why it is a red flag: The EITC is a common area for mistakes and fraud and the IRS knows it.

Recent audit rate: EITC claims have an audit rate of around 1.4%. In fact, according to the IRS, about 25% of EITC claims are paid in error.

How to protect against it: Make sure you meet the eligibility requirements and provide accurate information. Keep detailed records of your income, dependents, and other relevant factors.

Pro tip: Do not try it if you do not qualify. It is common for people to fraudulently claim the EITC and the IRS is always going after this low-hanging fruit.

CHAPTER 18
EARLY WITHDRAWALS FROM RETIREMENT ACCOUNTS

Why it is a red flag: Early withdrawals from retirement accounts will be data-matched and will get audited.

Recent audit rate: In my experience, early withdrawals have a 75% chance of being caught by the IRS.

How to protect against it: You can't, so just be ready for the tax burden.

Pro tip: If you need to dip into your 401k, have the administrator of the 401k withhold 30%. It will likely be a 20-30% tax plus a 10% penalty. If you need the money, you can take it but kiss 30-40% goodbye right away.

CHAPTER 19
HOBBY LOSSES

Why it is a red flag: Claiming losses for three out of five years will raise your DIF score and trigger a review by a human.

Recent audit rate: Losses for more than three years, have a high audit risk. It is hard to find the exact numbers, but I would estimate you have about a 25% chance of being audited if you claim a loss for more than three years.

How to protect against it: The IRS will want to see a profit motive and some work behind it. Do you have a business bank account, do you have any sales, do you market your product or service, etc.

Pro tip: Lots of businesses lose money at first and take a long time to make a profit. It's ok to not make money, you just need to be able to prove you are at least trying.

You can switch to a partnership tax return to lower your risk of an audit.

CHAPTER 20
LARGE CASH TRANSACTIONS

Why it is a red flag: Different from a cash business, cash deposits into your bank are reported to the IRS if they are over $10,000.

Recent audit rate: Large cash transactions do not affect your DIF score, but banks notify the government so try to avoid them when possible.

How to protect against it: Just be aware that if you deposit cash into a bank more than a few times a year, you could pop up on the radar of various government agencies.

Pro tip: Make sure your books are accurate in case someone comes looking. If you have a business, do not claim any "unreasonable" deductions because those combined with the large cash deposit might tip you over the scales for an audit.

CHAPTER 21
BUSINESS MEALS

Why it is a red flag: The IRS knows people exaggerate these numbers and they look for easy ones to audit.

Recent audit rate: Business meals that are large compared to income have an audit rate of about 3% from what I could find from various sources.

How to protect against it: Be reasonable compared to gross income and for the industry you are in.

Pro tip: Write notes on every receipt. If you get audited, the IRS agent may pick twenty out of two hundred receipts. If you have notes on the ones the agent picks, he or she will realize you run a tight ship and will likely move on instead of reviewing all two hundred receipts.

CHAPTER 22
CLAIMING HEAD OF HOUSEHOLD STATUS

Why it is a red flag: Claiming head of household status increases your refund and is easy to disprove.

Recent audit rate: Head of household claims have an audit rate of around 1.9% based on internet research.

How to protect against it: Make sure you are head of the household and have a dependent to claim.

Pro tip: If you can't agree who gets to claim your children, you are required to obey the court order. If your ex ignores the court order, then you should file early in the tax season and file first. This will allow you the head of household status. Your ex who is in the wrong will have to prove they should be head of household and without a court order, they cannot.

CHAPTER 23
CRYPTOCURRENCY TRANSACTIONS

Why it is a red flag: Crypto is a huge target for the IRS and easy to track based on large bank transfers.

Recent audit rate: Cryptocurrency transactions have an audit rate of approximately 3.4% but are going up.

How to protect against it: The IRS will be locking this down with a data match so I would not omit cryptocurrency profits.

Pro tip: Report crypto losses on tax returns because they will wash out some or even all of your gains. Keep in mind, if you hold the asset for more than one year, it is taxed at favorable capital gains tax rates of 0%, 15%, or 20%.

CHAPTER 24
LARGE MISCELLANEOUS DEDUCTIONS

Why it is a red flag: Large miscellaneous deductions show the IRS you do not have great record keeping.

Recent audit rate: It was hard to find the exact audit rate for high miscellaneous deductions. The risk of labeling things as miscellaneous in general is an IRS agent might think you have bad records and are an easy audit target.

How to protect against it: Try to break them down into categories and not just list them as miscellaneous.

Pro tip: If you are not exactly sure, do your best to break them down into categories such as supplies, tools, repairs, etc.

CHAPTER 25
TRUST TAX RETURNS WITH HIGH INCOME OR ASSETS

Why it is a red flag: Trust tax returns are sometimes used to illegally avoid tax, and the IRS knows it.

Recent audit rate: Trust tax returns currently have an audit rate of approximately 0.2%. This is likely to go up due to the increased IRS funding starting in 2023.

How to protect against it: Keep good records and be reasonable with expenses. Trusts can deduct expenses for lawyers, accountants, and administrators but if they go too high, they will get looked at more closely.

Pro tip: A non-revocable trust must be filed on a separate tax return, and you should use a tax accountant.

CHAPTER 26

S-CORPORATION TAX RETURNS WITH NO COMPENSATION FOR OFFICERS

Why it is a red flag: If you don't pay at least one officer a "reasonable salary," it is a huge red flag. It is easy for the DIF computer to run this number because it is listed on the front page of the S-corporation tax return.

Recent audit rate: S-corporation tax returns have an audit rate of approximately 0.4%. If the S-corporation has a profit and does not pay at least one officer with a W-2, the audit risk goes up to about 25% in my experience.

How to protect against it: The officers of an S-corporation must take a "reasonable salary." Look at line 7 of your S-corporation tax return. If that line is blank, talk to your tax accountant and ask them why.

Pro tip: Hire a payroll company to run your payroll and pay yourself with a W-2. You are required by the IRS to pay yourself a "reasonable salary."

CHAPTER 27
EXCESSIVE MEDICAL EXPENSES

Why it is a red flag: The IRS knows people who self-prepare might exaggerate these numbers because they are easy to make up.

Recent audit rate: Overall, medical expense deductions have an audit rate of approximately 1.8%.

How to protect against it: Keep records and receipts.

Pro tip: You can only deduct medical expenses if they are above 7.5% of your adjusted gross income.

For example, if you make $100,000 then you only can deduct anything over $7,500. There are some other limitations which are making medical expenses phase out as a deduction.

CHAPTER 28
OVERSTATING VEHICLE MILEAGE

Why it is a red flag: The IRS has access to a lot of data for "average annual mileage" for various industries. Mileage is easy for the DIF computer to read and compare to other tax returns in the same industry. If you stand out, it is easy to pull and send for audit.

Recent audit rate: Mileage claims have an audit rate of about 2.5% according to some published sources on the internet. Again, this is higher for mileage numbers above the standard range for your industry.

How to protect against it: Keep written logs of all business-related travel.

Pro tip: Invest in a phone app to track your miles. It will prompt you when you are driving with a simple question about the trip being business or personal.

CHAPTER 29

CLAIMING PERSONAL EXPENSES AS BUSINESS EXPENSES

Why it is a red flag: If you claim too many things on your business return, the IRS will see it as being higher than average.

Recent audit rate: Some sources say that expenses over 33% of gross revenue on a Schedule C will cause your DIF score to rise up high.

How to protect against it: Try to not go above 33% in expenses for more than a year or two on a Schedule C.

Pro tip: Think about switching to an S-corporation or partnership tax return.

CHAPTER 30
MISREPORTING INVESTMENT INCOME

Why it is a red flag: There is usually a data match if you sell an investment property. The IRS will receive the exact same tax form the escrow company gives you and will usually catch it.

Recent audit rate: Investment income misreporting has a published audit rate of about 2.6. I personally think it is much higher around 75% and going up with the increased IRS funding.

How to protect against it: You must always report investment property sales. If you sell an investment property, you only pay tax on the increase in value not on the sales price. If you sell a primary home you lived in, there are big tax breaks discussed in question #44.

Pro tip: If you sell something at a gain, try to also sell something at a loss in the same year. Try to separate the sales by tax year. Finally, try to sell things after holding onto them for at least one year so you get lower capital gains tax rates.

CHAPTER 31
LARGE TAX REFUNDS

Why it is a red flag: The IRS wants to make sure it is not fraud.

Recent audit rate: These are not audited in the typical fashion but are held up and looked at by a human before a large refund is issued.

How to protect against it: No need to protect against it, just be aware it may be reviewed by human eyes.

Pro tip: If your refund is held up, do not panic, it is normal. The good news is the IRS will pay you interest starting on day forty-five of it being held up.

CHAPTER 32
MULTIPLE STATES INCOME

Why it is a red flag: Many states such as California, New York, and New Jersey are auditing more and more tax returns because people are moving out of those states.

Recent audit rate: Multi-state income earners have an audit rate of about 2.1% unless you are in CA, NY, or NJ. If you are in one of those states, it is about a 1 in 10 chance in my opinion.

How to protect against it: Have proof that you don't live in these states such as pizza delivery bills, childcare statements, gym memberships, etc.

Pro tip: For multi-state returns, get with your tax accountant because there are ways you can legally avoid some of the higher tax rates in certain states.

CHAPTER 33

EXCESSIVE DEDUCTIONS FOR BUSINESS USE OF HOME

Why it is a red flag: The IRS is suspicious of home offices and can easily scan the office expense line from a schedule C business tax return.

Recent audit rate: Home office expense deductions have an audit rate of approximately 2.7%.

How to protect against it: Be reasonable and do your best to determine how much of your home is an office.

Pro tip: Measure your home office space accurately and come up with a percentage. This percentage can be applied to other utility bills such as electricity and gas. You can even take this percentage and apply it to a housekeeper or gardener.

Do not be scared to take these expenses but be reasonable.

CHAPTER 34
HIGH MORTGAGE INTEREST DEDUCTIONS

Why it is a red flag: The IRS gets the exact same mortgage interest statement you get.

Recent audit rate: Mortgages with a balance over $750,000 are looked at closely. I could not find numbers on this, but I estimate it to be about 66%.

How to protect against it: You can only use interest for up to $750,000 in mortgage debt. You need to determine the amount of interest that is for debt below $750,000 and exclude mortgage interest for debt above $750,000. It can be complicated, so if you owe over $750,000, hire a tax accountant.

Pro tip: You can write off 100% of mortgage interest for rental homes.

CHAPTER 35
FILING MULTIPLE AMENDED RETURNS

Why it is a red flag: Filing multiple amended returns makes you pop up on the radar.

Recent audit rate: Amended returns are usually either accepted or rejected. Multiple amended returns can cross paths and pique the curiosity of an IRS agent.

How to protect against it: Try not to file amended returns unless the juice is worth the squeeze.

Pro tip: If you are going to get back $200 for an amended return and you are self-employed making $500,000 a year, let sleeping dogs lie. If you are going to get back $200 for an amended return and you are a single parent making $50,000 from a W-2 job, then go for it.

CHAPTER 36
OVERSTATING TAX CREDITS

Why it is a red flag: Tax credits are free money, the IRS knows this and knows they are abused.

Recent audit rate: Tax credit claims have an audit rate of about 2.4% but this last tax season in 2023, they went much higher to around 5%. The audit insurance company I use said they have gone up a ton with the new IRS funding.

How to protect against it: This is blatant tax fraud and easy for the IRS to catch. Do not claim any tax credits unless you are actually entitled to them.

Pro tip: Energy credits are easily checked with what is called a correspondence audit. The IRS will mail you a letter asking for proof of eligibility. Keep your documents such as solar contracts, receipts, permits, and pictures for three years and be prepared to submit them if the IRS sends you an audit notice.

CHAPTER 37
CLAIMING TOO MANY CREDITS

Why it is a red flag: One credit makes sense but if you are getting three separate credits, the IRS may stop to make sure they are legitimate.

Recent audit rate: Multiple tax credit claims have a published audit rate of about 2.5%. This number is higher in my opinion for tax year 2023 and likely will be even higher in 2024.

How to protect against it: Do not take tax credits unless you want to have an elevated risk of being caught.

Pro tip: Take all credits you are entitled to and don't be afraid of a correspondence audit. However, be aware they are looked at more closely than they used to be.

CHAPTER 38

UNDERREPORTING YOUR HOUSEHOLD EMPLOYEE INCOME

Why it is a red flag: The IRS will data match this income based on tax forms.

Recent audit rate: I could not find exact data on this but for income that is reported to the IRS by employers, it is around 75-100% in my opinion.

How to protect against it: If you are a household employee such as a nanny, housekeeper, or personal assistant, ask your employer if they are going to report your income. If they are going to report it, then the IRS will know about it.

Pro tip: You can always take expenses against the money you made which will lower your taxes.

CHAPTER 39
FAILING TO REPORT STATE TAX REFUNDS

Why it is a red flag: Failing to report state tax refunds will catch up to you via…. You guessed it, a data match.

Recent audit rate: State tax refund reporting errors have a data match of up to 100%.

How to protect against it: Keep an eye out for tax forms and use them when getting your taxes done.

Pro tip: You can deduct state refunds and credits on your state taxes, so all is not lost.

CHAPTER 40
LARGE BUSINESS LOSSES

Why it is a red flag: Large business losses are different from repetitive business losses. A large loss, different from small losses over many years, is also a red flag.

Recent audit rate: Large business loss claims have an audit rate of approximately 2.9%.

How to protect against it: If you claim a huge business loss and it lowers your taxable income, this might cause the IRS to review the tax return with human eyes.

Pro tip: Certain size losses cause the DIF score to go up high enough to have the tax return looked at by human eyes. If you claim a big loss and it is legitimate, then you might get audited. If you have watertight records and are not afraid, then go for it. If not, then maybe lower your loss to a reasonable amount to avoid extra scrutiny.

CHAPTER 41

LARGE BUSINESS INCOME REPORTED ON PERSONAL RETURN

Why it is a red flag: Large business income on a schedule C is low-hanging fruit that a rookie IRS auditor can look at.

Recent audit rate: Hard to find exact data on this but I would estimate about 2%.

How to protect against it: If you make a ton of money your very first year that is great, but it is not normal. I would talk to my tax accountant about doing a partnership or S-corporation tax return.

Pro tip: An S-corporation will not only lower your audit risk, but it will save you 15.3% in tax.

CHAPTER 42
LARGE FOREIGN TAX CREDITS

Why it is a red flag: Foreign tax credits can easily be made up out of thin air because most countries don't have data matches with the US.

Recent audit rate: Foreign tax credit claims go up when the credit is large. For small credits, they are rarely audited.

How to protect against it: Keep your investment documents. Most foreign tax credits are from investments, and you will receive a 1099 from the investment administrator.

Pro tip: Foreign tax credits can lower your taxes. Make sure to ask your tax accountant if they know how to deal with foreign tax credits and if they are familiar with IRS form 1116.

CHAPTER 43
NON-COMPLIANCE WITH 1099 FORMS

Why it is a red flag: On your tax return, there is a box that asks if you need to issue 1099s. This is easy for the IRS to data match.

Recent audit rate: 1099 non-compliance has an audit rate of approximately 2.5% from what I could find from various sources.

How to protect against it: Always issue 1099s if you pay someone over $600. It can be complicated so if you are not good at it, hire a bookkeeper to do it for you.

Pro tip: If you use a third party to pay someone such as a credit card or Venmo, you do not have to issue 1099s. This is a huge money and time savings so, when possible, pay with Venmo or credit card.

CHAPTER 44
NOT REPORTING PRIMARY HOME SALES

Why it is a red flag: When you sell a primary home, the escrow company will usually issue a 1099S and this is a.... Wait for it...... A data match form!

Recent audit rate: If the escrow company issues a 1099S, this will be close to a 100% audit rate.

How to protect against it: Get the 1099S and give it to your tax accountant.

Pro tip: You can exclude $250,000 for single and $500,000 for married when selling a primary home. You can use a five-year lookback which means if you lived in the home for 730 days out of the last five years, it can be a primary home.

Tax planning when selling a home is important. Talk to your tax accountant before selling a home, because it can make a significant difference in your tax bill.

CHAPTER 45
CLAIMING CASUALTY LOSSES

Why it is a red flag: The IRS can perform a correspondence audit very easily and with minimal cost.

Recent audit rate: Casualty loss claims have an audit rate of approximately 2.4% according to what I could ind.

How to protect against it: Keep records and pictures of losses or damage.

Pro tip: There losses are hard to realize when filing your taxes due to several factors. Hire a tax accountant if you incur a large loss from theft or a disaster.

CHAPTER 46
FAILING TO REPORT STOCK SALES

Why it is a red flag: The IRS will data match any 1099s you receive from selling stocks.

Recent audit rate: The most recently published rate for stock sale non-reporting is 2.7%. However, I think it is much higher, around 50%.

In 2023, I received a lot of calls from self-filers who got an IRS letter for messing this up. My various clients owed the IRS anywhere from $10,000 to $65,000. Tax resolution can cost you anywhere from $1500-$10,000 so do not ignore 1099s.

How to protect against it: Report your stock sales on a schedule D because the IRS will get the info anyway.

Pro tip: It is important to pay attention to the 1099 form and see if the basis is or is not reported to the IRS. If the basis is reported to the IRS, you must use the basis on the 1099. If the basis is not reported to the IRS, you must do some digging to find the actual basis.

CHAPTER 47
FILING LATE VERSUS FILING ON TIME

Why it is a red flag: In my opinion, it makes no difference if you file late or on time. People think filing late helps avoid an audit, but this answer is to help dispel that myth.

Recent audit rate: The published audit rate for late tax returns and on-time tax returns is the same.

How to protect against it: Do not worry about it too much because there is no data to support which way is better.

Pro tip: If you are delaying filing your taxes because you cannot pay the tax, file your taxes, and let it go to collections. You can set up a payment plan and chip away at the balance. If you do not file, the tax owed and penalties will be much higher the longer you wait.

CHAPTER 48
OVERSTATING DEDUCTIONS FOR LEGAL FEES

Why it is a red flag: The IRS can compare your income to legal expenses and assess a risk factor with the DIF computer.

Recent audit rate: According to some people I have spoken to, unreasonably high legal expenses on a business tax return can have an audit rate of around 5%.

How to protect against it: Don't fudge numbers. Just because lawyers are expensive, you cannot make up unreasonable numbers to lower your income.

Pro tip: Do not include the entire expense of a divorce lawyer into a business expense as this is historically disallowed by the IRS.

CHAPTER 49

EXCESSIVE DEDUCTIONS FOR EQUIPMENT PURCHASES

Why it is a red flag: Depending on the amount, these purchases might need to be depreciated and this is easy for the IRS to disallow.

Recent audit rate: It is hard to determine the audit rate but typically if they are audited, the IRS will usually win on these.

How to protect against it: Know the difference between repairs and improvements or make sure your tax accountant knows.

Pro tip: Purchases over $5000 usually need to be depreciated over time.

CHAPTER 50
DISCREPANCIES BETWEEN FORMS

Why it is a red flag: This is a good one to close with because most audits come down to a data match. Remember, any official tax form you get, the IRS will in theory get as well!

Recent audit rate: Extremely high up to 100%. If you get a tax form, the IRS gets the same tax form. If they don't line up, they will likely audit you.

How to protect against it: Keep good track of your forms. If you get a 1099, report it and list expenses, do not just ignore it, and hope for the best.

Pro tip: As of the end of 2023, the IRS is about 12-18 months behind on audits even for data matching. Just because it has been a year, does not mean they are not going to come knocking. If they do send a letter, you can hire a good tax accountant and amend your tax return to claim expenses.

www.ingramcontent.com/pod-product-compliance
Lightning Source LLC
Chambersburg PA
CBHW071433210326
41597CB00020B/3773